101 Amazing Things to Do in Germany

© 2018 101 Amazing Things

All rights reserved. No part of this publication may be reproduced, distributed, or transmitted in any form or by any means, including photocopying, recording, or other electronic or mechanical methods, without the prior written permission of the publisher, except in the case of brief quotations embodied in critical reviews and certain other noncommercial uses permitted by copyright law.

Introduction

So you're going to Germany, huh? You are very lucky indeed! You are sure in for a treat because Germany is, without a doubt, one of the most special travel destinations on the face of the planet – and so underrated. It offers something for every visitor, so whether you are into exploring incredible German beers, having outdoor adventures in the Black Forest, or discovering the epic cool of Berlin, German will be a place you'll never forget.

This guide will take you on a journey from the major cities like Berlin, Munich, Hamburg, Hanover, and Cologne, as well as places in the German Alps, and the countryside of the Bavarian Forest.

In this guide, we'll be giving you the low down on:
- the very best things to shove in your pie hole, whether you need to want to chow down on currywurst on the street or you want to dine at a 3 Michelin Star restaurant
- incredible festivals, from electronic festivals with word famous headliners through to the Berlin International Film Festival

- the coolest historical and cultural sights that you simply cannot afford to miss like fairytale castles that inspired Disney movies, and world famous art galleries
- the most incredible outdoor adventures, whether you want to sled your way across a Toboggan run, or you fancy mountain biking in the depths of a German forest
- where to shop for authentic souvenirs so that you can remember your trip to Germany forever
- the places where you can party like a local and make new friends
- and tonnes more coolness besides!

Let's not waste any more time – here are the 101 most amazing, spectacular, and coolest things not to miss in Germany!

1. Visit a Hilltop Fairytale Castle in Bavaria

How often have you heard that a palace or a castle could have been ripped from the pages of a fairytale? Quite a few times, undoubtedly, but there is only one castle that can claim to have been the influence of Disney's castle in the Sleeping Beauty movie, and that is Neuschwanstein Castle, located in the south-west of Bavaria. It was commissioned by Ludwig II of Bavaria in the 19th century as a personal retreat for the reclusive King.

(Neuschwansteinstraße 20, 87645 Schwangau;

www.neuschwanstein.de)

2. Enjoy an Epic Karneval in Dusseldorf

When you think of carnival celebrations around the world, your mind will no doubt wander to the streets of Rio in Brazil with colourful parades, music, and dancing. Well, believe it or not, Karneval is also an extremely important celebration in Germany, and it's particularly vibrant on the streets of the neighbour cities, Dusseldorf and Cologne. In the Holy Week, you'll find a street parade that runs right throughout the cities, and everyone comes out to watch in their best costumes.

3. Take in the Views of the Rhine From Cologne Cathedral

If religious architecture is what does it for you, we have no doubt that you'll be in Seventh Heaven on your trip to Germany, and Cologne Cathedral is one church in particular that will leave you breathless. It was built all the way back in the mid 13th century, although parts of the church, such as its gigantic towers, were only completed in the late 19th century. If you are feeling energetic, we recommend climbing the 533 steps to the platform of the south tower, where you'll have wonderful views over Cologne and the River Rhine.

(Domkloster 4, 50667 Köln; www.koelner-dom.de/home)

4. Try a Traditional Bavarian Dessert, Germknodel

Aside for some great chocolate, Germany doesn't have much of a reputation when it comes to yummy sweet treats. But if you do have a sweet tooth, you'll be pleased to know that there are indeed some local desserts that you can tuck into, and when you find yourself in the southern region of Bavaria, something to try is Germknodel. This is a yeast dough dumpling that is filled with spiced plum jam and covered in melted butter and poppy seeds. It's the perfect thing for a cold day in Germany.

5. Explore the Street Art of Berlin

Berlin is widely recognised as one of the coolest cities in Europe, and this means that you can feel the lifeblood and creativity of the city absolutely everywhere that you go. Perhaps more than any other city on the continent, Berlin is absolutely covered in incredible street art that represents today's youth culture in Germany. There are quite a few tour companies that can take you around the city streets so you can get to know the ideas behind the art.

6. Fill Your Stomach at the Kolwitzplatz Farmers' Market

Berlin is a city with no shortage of great places where you can eat, but on a sunny day in the city, it's so much nicer to eat while strolling around than to sit down in a stuffy restaurant. That's why we are so enamoured by the Kowitzplatz Farmers' Market, which takes place each and every Thursday. Something really unique about this market is that it starts at noon, so the farmers have a chance to harvest their produce and sell it on the very same day. *(Kollwitzplatz, 10435 Berlin Prenzlaue)*

7. Take a Sobering Trip to the Sachsenhausen Concentration Camp Memorial

When in Germany, it's impossible not to face the country's history. Indeed, this is one of the primary reasons that people choose to visit Germany. If you are feeling strong and can face the horrors of the past, some people choose to visit former concentration camps, where Jews were imprisoned and murdered. The remaining buildings of the Sachsenhausen Concentration Camp now hold a museum where visitors can learn about this ugly part of German history.

(Str. der Nationen 22, 16515 Oranienburg; www.stiftung-bg.de/gums/en)

8. Feel Seduced by Hamburg's Miniatur Wunderland

Are you something of a geek? It is nothing to be ashamed of, and when we like to indulge our own inner geek, we make our way to Hamburg's Miniatur Wunderland to check out the world's largest model railway. The railway consists of 15,400 metres of track, divided into areas as far reaching as the Alps, Austria, America, Scandinavia, Switzerland, and Italy. Sections for France, England, and Australia are currently under construction.

(Kehrwieder 2-4/Block D, 20457 Hamburg; www.miniatur-wunderland.com)

9. Drown in Vats of Beer at Oktoberfest

It is no secret that Germans enjoy a glass of beer or ten, and this is never more evident than during the now world famous Oktoberfest, which is held in Munich each year from mid-September til the first weekend in October. Places all around the world host their own Oktoberfests these days, but for the real deal you need to venture to the heart of Bavaria. During the festival, you'll dress up, listen to Bavarian folk music, dance until you drop, and most importantly, try lots of incredible Bavarian beers.

10. Feel Festive at the Nuremberg Christmas Market

While it's true that Germany is cold and dark during the winter months, it's also a place with incredible Christmas spirit, and we never feel as festive as we do when we our wrapped up in our winter woollens, strolling the aisles of a good old fashioned German Christmas market. There are literally hundreds that you can go to, but Nuremberg Christmas Market might just be our number one. You can enjoy the special Nuremberg sausages, Nuremburg gingerbread, and buy the prettiest Christmas ornaments you've ever seen.

(www.christkindlesmarkt.de/en)

11. Tour the Allgau Cheese Route

You've heard of the Rhine Valley Wine Route, but what about a cheese route? Yep, in Germany you can even find this. The Allgau Cheese Route is located in the foothills of the Alps, and as you would probably expect, there are numerous Alpine dairies in the area that are very welcoming and let you tour the premises and taste all of their cheesy goodness. There's around 150km to explore, and you can do it by car, but we particularly love touring the area by bicycle in the spring and summer.

12. Breathe the Fresh Air of Englischer Garten

If you find yourself in Munich and you would like to escape the city streets for an afternoon, the Englischer Garten is the place to go to catch some fresh air and greenery. This is one of the largest city parks in all of Europe, rivalling Hyde Park and even Central Park in terms of size. Whether you want to walk across the green meadows, have a beer in the beer garden of the park, or even visit the park's Japanese teahouse, the choice is yours. *(www.muenchen.de/sehenswuerdigkeiten/orte/120242.html)*

13. Take in the Iconic Brandenburg Gate

When it comes to iconic landmarks in Germany, they don't get much more iconic than Berlin's Brandenburg Gate, an 18th century classical monument that used to mark the start of the city's limits. This is one of the most important places in European political history, with numerous demonstrations and protests taking place there throughout its history. It's also just one block from the Reichstag Building and the City Palace.

(Pariser Platz, 10117 Berlin;
www.berlin.de/sehenswuerdigkeiten/3560266-3558930-
brandenburger-tor.html)

14. Raise Your Voice at Berlin's Bearpit Karaoke

There is little more fun than heading to a karaoke bar with a group of friends and sucking the life out of an ABBA or Bon Jovi classic, but Berlin is a city that takes karaoke to the next level entirely. On Sunday afternoons in the summer months, a loudspeaker is set-up in the middle of Mauerpark, and local merrymakers take to the stage and belt out a tune or two in the open-air.

(www.bearpitkaraoke.com)

15. Visit the Schloss Vollrads Wine Estate

Although Germany is more famous for beer than wine, there is still a strong wine culture in Germany, and if you are a wine lover it can be very rewarding to get out into the wine country, and to explore some of the wineries and vineyards in the countryside. One of our favourites has to be the Vollrads Wine Estate. Situated in the Rheingau wine growing region, this estate has been producing wine for 800 years. They offer guided tours with tastings, a wine bar, and a restaurant.

(Vollradser Allee, 65375 Oestrich-Winkel; www.schlossvollrads.com)

16. Meet the Monks of Ettal Abbey

While you're in the southern region of Bavaria, there is so much more to explore than just Munich, and we suggest that you get out to some of the smaller towns like Ettal where the Ettal Abbey, a Benedictine Monastery with a community of 50 practicing monks can be found. The monks don't only support themselves with donations but with a number of business ventures on the premises. There is a distillery that sells herbal liqueur, a bookstore, an art publishing house, a cheese factory, and a hotel. *(Kaiser-Ludwig-Platz 1, 82488 Ettal; http://abtei.kloster-ettal.de/willkommen)*

17. Go Back in Time at the Pergamon Museum

The Pergamon Museum is Germany's largest art museum, and it's easy to spend multiple days inside and still want to come back and see more. Ancient art steals the show here, and museum is split between antiquities, art of the Middle East, and Islamic Art. We are particularly enamoured by the Antiquities with an incredible selection of sculpture, architecture, mosaics, bronzes, pottery, and jewellery from Ancient Greece and Rome.

(Bodestraße 1-3, 10178 Berlin; www.smb.museum/museen-und-einrichtungen/pergamonmuseum/home.html)

18. Dance, Dance, Dance at Melt! Festival

If electronic music is what does it for you, you might have already heard about Melt! Festival, which started in the late 90s and is already one of the most beloved open-air electronic festivals in the whole world. Each year, 20,000 people take to the German countryside so they can dance in the sunshine to some of the world's most acclaimed DJ talent. DJs that have previously played the festival include Girogio Moroder, Hercules & Love Affair, and Nina Kravitz.

(http://meltfestival.de/en)

19. Indulge a Bibliophile at Frankfurt Book Fair

Did you know that Frankfurt is home to the world's largest book fair? Well, if you are a book lover, it's a place that you need to know about and visit in mid-October when the fair takes place. Quite unbelievably, this book fair has a history that dates all the way back to the 17th century, and these days more than 250,000 people visit the fair each year. It's a great opportunity to buy some great books, go to some signings, and listen to readings from the world's best authors. Who said the printed word is dead?

(www.buchmesse.de/en/fbf)

20. Learn About Germany History at Deutsches Historiches Museum

The one part of German history that everybody knows about is the Second World War, and while it is a very important part of the national history, there is definitely more to German history than just this, and you can learn more about this great country at the Deutsches Historiches Museum in Berlin. Over 8000 historical objects tell the story of its beginnings and right up to the present day.

(Unter den Linden 2, 10117 Berlin; www.dhm.de)

21. Have a White Water Rafting Adventure on the Isar

As with any country, Germany is a place that has many sides to it. If the fancy takes you, you can sip on great German beers all day long, or if you want to get a little more active, you can immerse yourself in Germany's outstanding landscapes. If you want a true adrenaline rush, nothing quite beats the feeling of white water rafting along the river Isar. Not only is this a thrilling way to enjoy the outdoors, but it's a tradition in Bavaria that dates back to the 12th century.

22. Celebrate the Onset of Spring in Munich

Germany is a country with four distinct seasons, and this means that saying goodbye to the cold winter months and awakening to spring is always something of a celebration. And the best way to feel all the joy of spring is to join in with the festivities of the annual Munich Spring Festival. In true German fashion, one of the major attractions of the festival is beer gardens and beer tents, but there's also lots of fun for little ones with fairground rides and outdoor concerts.

(www.fruehlingsfest-muenchen.bayern/spring-fest-munich)

23. Visit the Birthplace of Beethoven

If you are a fan of classical music, Germany could be something of a pilgrimage site for you, as many of the most acclaimed composers in world history have come from Germany, and perhaps the most famous of them all is Ludwig Beethoven, born in Bonn in the latter half of the 18th century. It's a great idea to make it to Bonn so that you can visit the birthplace of the man himself, Beethoven House, which now serves as a museum dedicated to his life and works.

(Bonngasse 20, 53111 Bonn; www.beethoven-haus-bonn.de/sixcms/detail.php?template=portal_en)

24. Visit the World's Largest Museum of Science and Technology

If you are somebody who loves to hop from museum to museum, Germany truly has some of the best museums to be found anywhere on the planet. Take the Deutsches Museum in Munich, for example, which is the largest science museum in the whole world. And this is not a stuffy museum where everything is kept behind glass partitions. It's very interactive so that kids can learn and enjoy about the laws of nature, the cosmos, robotic technology, and lots more besides.

(Museuminsel 1, 80538 München; www.deutsches-museum.de)

25. Discover Incredible Old Master Paintings at Alte Pinakothek

If you are an arts lover, you might be tempted to visit France or Italy before you head to Germany, but we have no doubt that arts lovers will feel very much rewarded on a trip to Germany. Perhaps our favourite gallery in the whole country is Alte Pinakothek in Munich, one of the oldest galleries in the world, with a wonderful collection of paintings from the Old Masters like Rubens, van Dyck, Giotto, Titan, and more.

(Barer Str. 27, 80333 München; www.pinakothek.de)

26. Try a Type of German Meatloaf, Leberkase

If you are a meat lover, the culinary scene in Germany is sure to impress you. Of course, there are many types of sausages to be enjoyed all over the country, but something less well known and very delectable is Leberkase, which can be thought of as a kind of German meatloaf. This is mostly found in the south of the country, and can contain a mix of corned beef, pork, bacon, and onions. It is often served with freshly baked what rolls, mustard, and pickles.

27. Explore the Wildlife at Hellabrunn Zoo

If you are an animal lover, you will probably debate whether you should visit zoos on trips away or not. But one zoo that has consistently great reputation for animal care is the Hellabrun Zoo in Munich. This is widely considered as one of the very best zoos in Europe, and it has some unique features. Instead of set behind wires or glass, this zoo uses moats to separate most of the animals from the visitors, and the zoo is organised by geographical aspect rather than by animal species.

(Tierparkstr. 30, 81543 München; www.hellabrunn.de/en)

28. Visit the Palace of Former Bavarian Monarchs, Munich Residenz

Bavaria is a part of Germany with a long and illustrious history; it enjoyed huge amounts of power and riches throughout many centuries, and this makes it a great place to visit palaces and castles. One of the grandest places has to be the Munich Residenz, the former residence of the Bavarian monarchs. The first buildings on the site were constructed in 1385, and now comprise ten courtyards and 130 rooms, filled with incredible architectural details and opulent furnishings.

(Residenzstraße 1, 80333 München; www.residenz-muenchen.de)

29. Eat the Best Burger of Your Life in Hamburg

While hamburgers are thought of as a singularly American thing, meat lovers might be interested to know that the original inspiration for the humble hamburger was born in the Germany city of Hamburg. And so, of course, it's important to chow down and eat a burger while you're in the city. For our money, the best spot for this is Duff's Burger, a place where burgers are everything they should be and then some. We highly recommend the Farmer Burger, comprising a beef patty, marinated bacon, cheese, and eggs.

(Karolinenstraße 2, 20357 Hamburg; www.dulfsburger.de)

30. Be Wowed by a 14 Century Lutheran Church in Hanover

When you think of church architecture, you might think of Italy and France before you think of Germany, but this country is absolutely packed full of gorgeous church architecture, and one of the churches we wouldn't miss is Marktkirche, a 14th century Lutheran church in Hanover that exemplifies the North German neo-Gothic style. The exposed brick gives this church a very unique look and feel.

(Hanns-Lilje-Platz 2, 30159 Hannover; http://marktkirche-hannover.de)

31. Tuck Into Some Veal Schnitzel

There are certain foods that are so quintessentially German that it would be crazy to leave the country before you try them. For a start, there is veal schnitzel. Schnitzel is sometimes known as milanesa in other countries, and it basically means that a piece of meat is pounded down so that it becomes a thin slice. That slice of meat is then coated in breadcrumbs and fried. This can be done with chicken or pork, but we recommend veal for a taste of true German decadence.

32. Sip on Innovative Craft Beers at Vagabund Brauerei

Germany is a country well known for its incredible beer culture, and you certainly won't have a hard time finding a decent pint of beer or a microbrewery in the country. One of our enduringly favourite spots would have to be Vagabund Brauerei, a microbrewery that prides itself on a selection of around ten innovative brews. While the beer is most certainly delicious, our favourite thing about this place is that you are allowed to bring your own food inside.

(Antwerpener Str. 3, 13353 Berlin; www.vagabundbrauerei.com)

33. Tour the Rococo Interiors of Nymphenburg Palace

Normally when you want to visit grand palaces and buildings, the capital city of a country is the place to be, but we think that Munich outdoes Berlin when it comes to grand historical attractions, and this is, of course, because Munich is the capital of Bavaria, which has such a long and important history. One of the buildings not to miss in Munich is Nymphenburg Palace, which acted as the summer residence of Bavarian monarchs for centuries. It was completed in 1664, commissioned by Prince Ferdinand Maria who built the palace for his wife. *(Schloß Nymphenburg 1, 80638 München; www.schloss-nymphenburg.de/englisch/palace)*

34. Stroll the Aisles of a 200 Year Old Market, Viktualienmarkt

For us, one of the loveliest ways to get to know a new place is by strolling the aisles of its markets. This way, you get the chance to see local life in action, and the most famous market in Munich is the Viktualienmakt, which has a history of 200 years. The market is open every day apart from Sunday, and we advise getting there early to catch the best produce. It's situated in a public square, and you'll be able to find flowers, spices, cheese, fish, fruits and veggies, juices, and lots more.

(Viktualienmarkt 3, 80331 München; www.muenchen.de/rathaus/Stadtverwaltung/Kommunalreferat/ma rkthallen/viktualienmarkt.html)

35. Get to Grip With Bavarian Culture at the Bavarian National Museum

Who doesn't love to look at beautiful things? We certainly do, and that's why we think that the Bavarian National Museum is one of the most underrated treasures of Germany's museum scene, and in our opinion it has one of the greatest collections of decorative arts in Europe. Inside you will find objects from the Gothic, Renaissance, Rococo, and Baroque periods, with a huge range of items such as textiles, glass paintings, carved ivory, tapestries, shrines, and much more.

(Prinzregentenstraße 3, 80538 München; www.bayerisches-nationalmuseum.de)

36. Indulge a Chocaholic at Imhoff-Schokoladenmuseum

There are two kinds of people in this world. People who love chocolate above everything else, and people who we have no desire to know or understand. If you're also a major chocaholic, an attraction that is sure to appeal to you is the Imhoff-Shokoladenmuseum in Cologne, a museum that tells the story of chocolate right from its beginnings with the Olmecs, Mayas, and Aztecs. Special features include a greenhouse with cacoa trees, and a three metre high chocolate fountain.

(Am Schokoladenmuseum 1A, 50678 Köln;
www.schokoladenmuseum.de/en)

37. Enjoy a Slice of Central Asia at Tajikistan Tearoom

One of the last things you would expect to find in the middle of Berlin is a tearoom inspired by Central Asia, right? Well, guess what? It's there, and it's just waiting to be visited. Actually, this tearoom was donated by the Soviet Republic of Tajikistan to East Germany in the 1970s, but it still serves up Asian teas and Russian food today. The interior has a total Persian style, with intricately carved wooden pillars and lush textiles throughout. *(Oranienburger Str. 27, 10117 Berlin; www.tadshikische-teestube.de)*

38. Escape City Life at the Berlin Botanical Garden

As one of the most happening capital cities in the world, Berlin might just be a little bit overwhelming at times. But Berlin, like most German cities, is actually very green, and this means that when you need to escape the hustle and bustle of city life, you can simply make your way to the

Berlin Botanical Garden. It covers over 43 hectares of land, and there's more than 22,000 plant species around the gardens, including giant water lilies, orchids, and carnivorous plants.

(Königin-Luise-Straße 6-8, 14195 Berlin; www.bgbm.org/en/home)

39. Zone Out in a Futuristic Spa, Liquidrom

When you're on holiday, it's the time to relax, unwind, and let the weight of the world fall from your shoulders. And what better way to do so than with a spa day? Of course, you can find various spas all over Germany, but one that we think is particularly special is a futuristic spa called Liquidrom, located in Berlin. The centrepiece of the spa is a giant saltwater pool, which you can float in, and forget the stresses of everyday life.

(Möckernstraße 10, 10963 Berlin; www.liquidrom-berlin.de/de/index.php)

40. Have an Artsy Morning at Berggruen Museum

Although the Berggruen Collection was only opened to the public in 1996, it certainly does contain one of the most impressive collections of modern art in the world. All of the names you want to see are exhibited here: from Pablo Picasso to Henri Matisse, and Paul Klee to Aberto Giacometti. The museum is particularly strong on Picasso, with over 120 works by the master that represent a broad survey of his life and work.

(Schloßstraße 1, 14059 Berlin; www.smb.museum/en/museums-institutions/museum-berggruen/home.html)

41. Fill Your Stomach at Cologne's Street Food Festival

Let's face it, foodie travellers might not have Germany at the top of their must-visit list unless they are serious fans of sausage and potatoes, but scratch the surface and you can actually find a culinary scene that is getting more and more exciting with each year that passes. One place where you can experience lots of yummy treats is the annual Cologne Street Food Festival, which is hosted every year in May. Some of the delights on offer include bahn mi Vietnamese sandwiches, pulled pork, wild garlic sausages, and lots more deliciousness besides.

(http://street-food-festival.de/#street-food-festival)

42. Go Mountain Biking in the Franconian Forest

There is lots of gorgeous nature to be explored in Germany, and one of the most exhilarating ways to get to know the countryside is to get on your bike and pedal away. If you want a gentle cycling experience, you can cycle along the Rhine river, but for something altogether more exciting, why not head to the Franconian Forest and a have a mountain biking adventure where there just so happens to be 300km of mountain bike trails?

43. Search for Vintage Treasures at Arkonaplatz

As you stroll the streets of Berlin, you can't help but notice that the local people are very trendy indeed. And if you would like to take home a slice of that Berlin cool with you, we would like to recommend Arkonaplatz, a weekly vintage flea market that is held every Sunday on a leafy square in the city. There is a huge emphasis placed on vintage fashions, but you'll also be able to find vintage furniture, art prints, jewellery, and more.

(www.troedelmarkt-arkonaplatz.de)

44. Catch a Show During Munich Ballet Week

For lovers of high culture, there are plenty of opportunities to watch opera and ballet shows in Germany, and one of the best places to catch a grand performance would certainly be the Munich National Theatre, which opened way back in 1818. This stage hosts incredible performances throughout the year, but it really comes to life during April, when it hosts Munich Ballet Week. Each year, there are performances from both local and international ballet companies.

(www.staatsoper.de/en/staatsballett/ballet-festival-week.html)

45. Eat in Dusseldorf's Revolving Restaurant, Gunnewig

If you make it to Dusseldorf, something that you will surely see on the city's horizon is Rheinturm, a telecommunications tower with a height of 240 metres. But there is more to this tower than meets the eye because inside you can find a glamorous revolving restaurant. Gunnewig Rheinturm Restaurant has a height of 170 metres, and eating there gives you incredible views over the whole city and beyond. It's the perfect spot for a special celebration.

(Stromstraße 20, 40212 Düsseldorf; www.guennewig.de/rheinturm-duesseldorf/restaurant-top-180)

46. Stroll Through the Botanical Gardens of Wilhelma

Stuttgart is one of the most underrated destinations in Germany, and we think it's well worth visiting if only to pay a visit to the Wilhelma Zoological and Botanical Gardens. This is one of the more unique zoo set-ups that we have ever seen. Instead of being set behind glass, the animals are separated with ditches that they can't traverse. Also, the botanical gardens here are just as important, and you'll find 7000 species of plants from every climate on the planet. This is one that nature lovers shouldn't miss. *(Wilhelmapl. 13, 70376 Stuttgart; www.wilhelma.de)*

47. Have a Perfect Sunday Morning at Hamburg's Fischmarkt

Sundays are made for strolling in the outdoors, perhaps by the edge of the river, and eating a few bites of something delicious. Ad that's why you will always find us at the Sunday Fischmarkt when we are in Hamburg. You do need to be an early bird to get to this market, because it's only in operation from 7-9:30am on Sundays, but it's well worth dragging yourself out of bed for a fresh fish sandwich and a strong coffee along the bank of the Elbe river.

48. Enjoy the Taste of Stuttgart, Gaisburger Marsch

Germany is one of the larger countries in Europe, and this means that as you travel from city to city, you can experience a totally different culture, and that goes for the food culture too. Stuttgart is one of the most underrated cities in Germany, but we recommend that you visit if only to tuck into a steaming bowlful of Gaisburger Marsch, the local version of a beef stew. The cubes of beef are cooked in beef broth with potatoes and spätzle, a kind of soft egg noodle.

49. Hit a Few Golf Balls at Hartl in Bavaria

If your idea of a great vacation involves heading to the nearest golf course and hitting a few golf balls, you're in luck because Germany plays host to some of the finest golf greens in Europe. Of course, there are so many golf courses that appeal to all kinds of golfers no matter if

you're a total beginner or an expert. But the Hartl Golf
Resort is known for its testing golf tracks, and this is one
you visit to really challenge yourself and your golfing skills.
(Kurallee 1, 94086 Bad Griesbach im Rottal; www.hartl.de/en)

50. Shop for Goodies at Hamburg's Flohschanze Market

While you are in Germany, you will no doubt want to
allocate some time to shopping for some special items so
that you can always remember your trip. And where better
for some leisurely weekend shopping than at Hamburg's
flea market, Flohschanze Market? It takes place every
Saturday and draws and enthusiastic local crowd. We love
the new items are strictly prohibited from being sold, so
you know that the vintage art, jewellery, or furniture you
find will always be the real deal.
(Neuer Kamp 30, 20357 Hamburg)

51. Be Stunned by 16th Century Heidelberg Castle

Looking high over the city of Heidelberg is the gorgeous
and imposing Heidelberg Castle, one of the most
important Renaissance structures north of the Alps. The

original structure was created in the early 14th century, but it has been added to and destroyed so many times that different parts of the castle belong to different eras and architectural styles, with most of the work taking place in the 16th century. We also recommend the Apothecary Museum on the site of the castle.

(Schlosshof 1, 69117 Heidelberg; www.schloss-heidelberg.de)

52. Have a Night of Decadent Cocktails at Clockers in Hamburg

If you find yourself in Hamburg on a Friday night and you aren't quite sure where's the best place for a cocktail or two, we would love to recommend a secret among the local population called Clockers. This underground cocktail bar has the feel of a magical forest with moss growing all over the walls. But this place isn't all show – the cocktails are every bit as magical as the interiors. They also have produce their own gin, and have regular gin tastings, which we highly recommend.

(Paul-Roosen-Straße 27, 22767 Hamburg;
http://clockers.hamburg/de/home)

53. Have a Glass or Two at Stuttgart Wine Festival

Although Germany is a country that has achieved greater acclaim for its delicious beers than it wines, we don't think that wine lovers will feel disappointed on a trip to Germany whatsoever, and there are plenty of wine regions to explore around the country. And a place that offers endless exploration of German wines is the Stuttgart Wine Festival, which is hosted each year at the beginning of September. Over 120 vendors sell their wares, with guided tastings and food pairings.

(www.stuttgarter-weindorf.de/english)

54. Discover Artsy Germany at Staedel in Frankfurt

Lovers of arts and culture might think that they should spend all of their time in Berlin, but actually there is a very vibrant arts culture to be discovered right around Germany, and the number one gallery of Frankfurt is certainly Staedel, with 2700 paintings, over 100,000 drawings, and around 600 sculptures to peruse. Some of the artists on display include Sandro Boticelli, Edgar Degas, and Johannes Vermeer.

55. Take in a Football Match at Allianz Arena, Munich

If you are a sports lover, you certainly won't be alone in Germany. This country is absolutely crazy about football, and one of the best loved teams in Germany is definitely FC Bayern Munich. Catching a live match is a once in a lifetime experience for sports fans. The Allianz Arena in Munich can contain 75,000 spectators at a time, so the atmosphere inside the stadium has to be experienced to be believed. It's also possible to take an arena tour.

(https://allianz-arena.com/de)

56. Be Stunned by Zwinger, a Baroque Palace in Dresden

When it comes to grand palaces of Europe, we think that Zwinger in Dresden might just be one of the grandest of them all, and yet this is not a building that is known by most people in the world unless they have a particular interest in Baroque architecture. While the outside of the palace is extremely impressive, the interiors have a lot to offer as well, with many art collections. We are particularly enamoured by the Dresden porcelain collection, which is one of the largest ceramics collections in the world.

(Sophienstraße, 01067 Dresden; www.der-dresdner-zwinger.de/en/home)

57. Have a Decadent Slice of Black Forest Gateau

One of the German desserts that has found fame around the world is the Black Forest Gateau, which in German is Schwarzwalder Kirschtorte, and it is named after the strong liqueur that is made from sour cherries in the Black Forest region. This decadent cake is made of multiple layers of rich chocolate sponge, which are sandwiched with fresh whipped cream, fresh cherries, sour cherries, and the famous cherry liquor soaks right throughout the cake.

58. Stay in Your Own Private Igloo at Iglu-Dorf

On your trip to Germany, you probably intend on staying in hotels, hostels, and guesthouses, and while there's absolutely nothing wrong with that, there are some more exciting accommodation choices to be found throughout Germany. For example, how darn cool would it be to stay in an igloo? Yeh, you heard us right. Iglu-Dorf in the

German Alps is a place where you can rent an igloo for the night and have a true winter experience.

(Zugspitze, 82475 Garmisch-Partenkirchen; www.iglu-dorf.com/de/standorte/zugspitze)

59. Visit a German Island in the Baltic Sea, Rugen

The island of Rugen is a place known by many German holidaymakers, but it hasn't gained the international reputation that it so deserves. Of course, when you think of Germany, it's unlikely that you think of island destinations, but Germany even has this, and Rugen is, in fact, Germany's largest island. Most people visit to explore the wonderful Jasmund National Park, which is beloved because of its white cliffs that provide incredible views out to the ocean.

60. Take in the Views of Hanover From New Town Hall

Although it was only completed in 1913, the New Town Hall is one of the most important buildings in the whole of Hanover, and it's certainly one of the most striking. This building took twelve years to build, and it was and still is the seat of the Mayor of Hanover, where political sessions are still held today. We highly recommend ascending to the dome of the Town Hall, where you will experience incredible views out over the city.

Trammplatz 2, 30159 Hannover;

61. People Watch in the Beer Gardens of Mauerpark

Yes, Berlin is a busy capital city, but one of the most pleasing things about this city is that there are just so many green spaces dotted around the city. Even better, some of these green spaces have beer gardens where you can sip on glorious German beers in the Berlin sunshine. Cut to the beer gardens of Mauerpark. There is even a beach bar at this particular beer garden, and we can think of no better destination for a mid-week evening in the city.

(Bernauer Str. 63-64, 13355 Berlin; www.mauersegler-berlin.de)

62. Learn About the Horrors of Nazi Germany at Topography of Terror

Berlin is a city that has many difficult stories to tell about its past, and particularly during the Nazi regime that caused the deaths of millions of people. Berlin was where the central offices of the Gestapo were based, and it's at this location that you can find the Topography of Terror, a museum dedicated to explaining the terror of the time, where it came from, how it took hold, and what strategies of terror were implemented. This museum is free to visit. *(Niederkirchnerstraße 8, 10963 Berlin; www.topographie.de)*

63. Take the Alpine Railway to Germany's Highest Mountain

Zugspitze is the highest peak in Germany, belonging to the Wetterstein Mountains. You might think that you need to have an incredible fitness level to be able to traverse this mountain and take in the local scenery, but that is not necessarily the case thanks to the Bavarian Zugspitze Railway. This railway line will take you 2650 metres above level, making it the highest railway line in Germany, and the third highest in Europe. Needless to say, the vistas from the top are breathtaking.

64. Discover Freaky Industrial Objects at Design Panoptikum

Berlin is without a doubt one of the best cities for museum going in all of Europe. There are incredible national museums and galleries, but beyond this, we love to visit some of the hidden treasures of the city's museum scene, like the Design Panoptikum. This museum is dedicated to Extraordinary Objects pertaining to industrial design. Some of the oddities you'll see include iron lungs and film projectors.

(Torstraße 201, 10115 Berlin; www.designpanoptikum.com)

65. Enjoy the Scenic Journey on the Central Rhine Railway

If we have a choice of transport options, we always love to take the train Germany. Not only are European trains typically very comfortable, but they are an attraction in their own right, and you get to enjoy some incredibly scenic landscapes as you chug along. One of the train journeys that we take again and again is from Mainz to Koblenz. It showcases the calm waters of the River Rhine and the slopes of the Rhine Valley wine growing region.

66. Start the Day Right With Some Schwarzbrot

As the saying goes, breakfast is the most important meal of the day, and this is never more true than when you are travelling and you need all the energy that you can muster for lots of sightseeing and activities. And when we're in Germany, we always like to begin the day with a hearty helping of Schwarzbrot. Traditionally, Schwarzbrot is a bread made with at least 90% rye whole grain, making it very dark and dense. Simply served with butter, it's a filling breakfast to give you energy until lunchtime.

67. Pay Your Respects at Berlin's Holocaust Memorial

If you visit Berlin, something that you have to contend with is the country's past, and many people wish to pay their respects and honour the lives of the people lost in the Holocaust when visiting Germany. One of the places that is most popular for this, and indeed designed for this purpose, is Berlin's Holocaust Memorial. This is a very unique memorial installation because you can actually walk through it, immerse yourself in it, and learn about the people who lost their lives during the rule of Nazi Germany.

(Cora-Berliner-Straße 1, 10117 Berlin; www.stiftung-denkmal.de/startseite.html)

68. Take a Tour of the Ziegler Whisky Distillery

If you are a whisky lover, you are probably already familiar with varieties of this tipple from places like Ireland and Scotland, but German also produces some great whisky too. If you would like to learn more about Germany's own whisky culture, it can be worth finding your way to the Ziegler Distillery in Franconia. The difference with their whisky is that it's quite fruity with notes of whisky and wine. It's also possible to take a tour of the distillery and try some of the good stuff.

(www.brennerei-ziegler.de/en/whisky.html)

69. Tour One of Germany's Most Important Buildings, Reichstag Building

As the seat of the German Parliament, there is absolutely no question that the Reichstag building is one of the most important structures to be found anywhere in Germany, but it's not just an important building, it's also a very attractive one. Parts of the building have been destroyed and rebuilt because of the war, and these days many people visit to ascend to the building's impressive glass dome. You should be aware that you need to register two days in advance to visit the glass dome and roof terrace. *(Platz der Republik 1, 11011 Berlin;*

www.bundestag.de/besuche/architektur/reichstag)

70. Watch a Movie at the Berlin International Film Festival

If you are a huge movie buff, the Berlin International Film Festival will probably already be on your radar, because it is one of the most celebrated film festivals anywhere in the world. It takes place every February, and we strongly suggest battling the Berlin winter and making it to the German capital at this time if you love movies. As well as hundreds of movie premieres from around the world, you can attend talks, workshops, and panel discussions with industry leaders.

(www.berlinale.de/en)

71. Chow Down on Incredible Japanese Food in Dusseldorf

Something that you might not know about the unassuming small city of Dusseldorf is that it has one of the densest populations of Japanese people outside of Japan, which gives the city a unique feel. For a start, it plays host to the largest Buddhist temple in the whole of Europe, and secondly, it means that you can chow down on incredible Japanese food in the Japantown area. Some of the most acclaimed Japanese restaurants in Dusseldorf are Takumi, Naniwa, and Yabase.

72. Be Transported to Ancient Egypt at Neues Museum

The Neues Museum originally opened all the way back in the mid 19th century, but after being bombed during the Second World War it was left in disrepair, and only reopened very recently in 2009. This museum is dedicated to showcasing incredible finds from ancient cultures all around the world, and is particularly strong on Ancient Egypt.

(Bodestraße 1-3, 10178 Berlin; www.smb.museum/museen-und-einrichtungen/neues-museum/home.html)

73. Rock Til You Drop at Rock am Ring

These days, the summer festival circuit tends to dedicate itself to electronic and club music, but what if you're a rocker at heart? Well, Germany has just the festival for you: Rock am Ring. Rock am Ring takes place at the beginning of June at an old airbase, where thousands of people who live music rock out to the most incredible bands, from soft indie to thrash metal. Acts that have performed at Rock am Ring include Slipknot, The Prodigy, Kings of Leon, and Rammstein.

(www.rock-am-ring.com)

74. Tuck Into Mettbroetchen in Cologne

It's no secret that Germany is a nation full of meat lovers, but that extends way beyond a spot of sausage, and one of the most unique meat dishes to be found anywhere in the country is Mettbroetchen, a dish that hails from Cologne. This is basically a preparation of minced pork with salt, pepper, caraway seeds, garlic, and chopped onion. Sounds nice enough, right? Well, something you should know is that the meat is entirely raw and served on bread. Worth trying once?

75. Wave a Rainbow Flag at Berlin Pride

Berlin is one of the most inclusive places in the whole of Europe, and we think that LGBT people should feel safe there, and will have a great time partying at the bars and clubs across the capital city. And if you really want to feel your oats, you shouldn't miss out on Berlin Pride, which takes place at the end of June each year. This is a fun festival with lots of parties, and it all culminates in a colourful street parade watched by thousands upon thousands of people.

(http://csd-berlin.de)

76. Hike Around Lake Eibsee

For lovers of the great outdoors, Germany is absolutely crammed full of picturesque landscapes, and when we just want to relax in nature, we head down to Lake Eibsee in Bavaria, which lies about an hour south of Munich. The waters of the lake are so dazzlingly blue that it can seem as though you are looking at a postcard image, and it's the ideal place for a brisk hike on a sunny day. There is a 7.5km marked trail that starts in front of the Eibsee Hotel.

77. Discover a World of Treasures at Grunes Gewolbe

If your idea of a great holiday is to immerse yourself in art, culture, and beauty, then you absolutely cannot miss Grunes Gewolbe in Dresden. This museum dates all the way back to 1723, and it contains the largest collection of treasures in Europe, with a huge variety of objects from the Baroque to the Classical world, and much more. Highlights of the collections include a cherry stone from the 16th century with 185 faces carved into it, and the Dresden Green Diamond, and incredibly valuable and unique jewel.

(Residenzschloss, Taschenberg 2, 01067 Dresden; www.skd.museum)

78. Discover Berlin Fashions at Nowkoelln Flowmarkt

There is absolutely no doubt that Berliners are some of the trendiest people on the planet, and while you're in Berlin it can be a great idea to take to the streets and shop for some of that Berlin style. The ultimate place to do this is Nowkoelln Flowmarkt, a hipster-heavy flea market that takes place twice a month and offers the most stylish second-hand threads at very affordable prices. *(Maybachufer 31, 12047 Berlin; www.nowkoelln.de)*

79. Warm Yourself From the Inside Out With a Plate of Sauerbraten

We cannot pretend that visiting Germany in the wintertime is without challenges, but on the plus side you have the opportunity to take in the wintry landscapes of the country, and take in some delicious German comfort food at the same time. When we need to be warmed through from the inside out, our go-to German dish is Sauerbraten, which is the German take on a pot roast. The meat is usually beef, and it is marinated for many days in a mix of vinegar, herbs, spices, and seasonings, and served with red cabbage and potato dumplings.

80. Get a Taste of Africa at International Africa Festival

You probably didn't go all the way to Germany to learn about African culture, but in our multi-cultural world, even this is possible in the 21st century. The festival is hosted every August in a little known city in northern Bavaria called Wurzburg. So far, more than 6500 musicians from 56 countries across Africa have performed at this festival, making it one of the largest festivals dedicated to African culture in the world.

(www.africafestival.org/en)

81. Enjoy a Cocktail With a View at Klunkerkranich

The summer months in Berlin are so much fun, and one of the best ways to enjoy the sunshine and the long evenings is by taking to a rooftop bar. Our favourite spot for a cocktail with a view would have to be Klunkerkranich, which is a bar on top of a huge parking garage. It's unassuming, a little bit grungy, and most of all, it's totally Berlin. It's a lovely place for a drink and a chat in the early evening, and there are normally parties and DJs playing into the night if you want the real Berlin drinking experience.

(Neukölln Arcaden, Karl-Marx-Straße 66, auf dem obersten Parkdeck, 12043 Berlin; www.klunkerkranich.org)

82. Ski in the Sunshine at Zugspitze

Germany is very much a country of extremes. It can be baking hot in the summer months, and freezing cold in the winter. While the summer might seem more obviously pleasant for a trip to Germany, the winters has its draws too, and particularly if you are into winter sports. Zugspitze is the highest mountain in Germany, and it's also a very popular ski destination because of the amount of sunshine it gets, and the snow it has for eight months of the year.

83. Discover Roman Antiquities at the Romano-Germanic Museum

Something you may not be aware of is that the city of Cologne was at one point a Roman settlement, and you can learn about this aspect of the city's history, and Roman life in general at Cologne's Romano-Germanic Museum. This is more than just a museum with objects behind glass. In the basement, you can find an incredible reconstruction of a Roman villa, and the Dionysus mosaic in its original location.

(Roncalliplatz 4, 50667 Köln; www.roemisch-germanisches-museum.de/Startseite)

84. Say Hi to the Animals at Berlin Zoological Garden

Travelling with kids is a double edged sword. On the one hand, you want to provide your kids with incredible memories that they can carry with them for years to come, but on the other hand, it's just really difficult to keep young children entertained. But a day at the zoo is always a good idea, and will keep the whole family happy. So thank goodness for the Berlin Zoological Garden, the oldest zoo in Germany. Inside the park, you can get close to Giant Pandas, penguins, red kangaroos, and more.

(Hardenbergplatz 8, 10787 Berlin; www.zoo-berlin.de/en)

85. Eat at a Hamburg Restaurant With 3 Michelin Stars

We know that not everyone has the means to eat out at fine dining restaurants every night while they're on holiday, but we think that you need to have at least one incredible dining experience while you're in Germany. And honestly, the definition of fine dining is The Table in Hamburg, a restaurant with no fewer than 3 Michelin stars. There is just one large table that can seat 20 guests, and every diner has a view into the open kitchen.

(Shanghaiallee 15, 20457 Hamburg; www.thetable-hamburg.de)

86. Sip on Gluhwein Before Christmas

You will never feel quite as festive as when you are strolling the aisles of a German Christmas market and chomping on spiced gingerbread cookies. And although it's certainly cold in Germany throughout December, we think that Gluhwein offers the perfect opportunity to keep toasty and warm. This is red wine that is head through with orange juice, and spices such as cinnamon and cloves, and we think that it's the taste of the Christmas season.

87. Go Sledding on Germany's Longest Toboggan Run

Call us crazy but we think that the depths of winter can be a great time to visit Germany. For a start, you get to experience all of the cool winter activities that you can't try out in the summer. On Wallberg Mountain, you can find Germany's longest and most challenging natural sledding run, which extends for 6.5km. We love nothing more than to put on our snow goggles, and speed through this super-fun Toboggan run with friends.

88. Feel Cologne's Creativity at CityLeaks Urban Festival

Cologne is a very young city, with a huge student population, and a creative heartbeat running throughout. One of the best ways to experience all the creativity of Cologne is by visiting during September for the CityLeaks Festival, a celebration of dynamic urban art through a huge collection of media. You'll get to check out some graffiti work, street sculptures, performance art, and more. *(http://cityleaks-festival.com)*

89. Indulge a Cheese Lover With a Bowl of Obatzda

Put a plate of cheese in front of us, and we are happy as a clam. If you love cheese just as much as we do, Germany is a wonderful choice of country to visit. As well as many local cheeses, there are also some unique cheese dishes to try, and one of the most delicious is something called obatzda that hails from Bavaria. This is a mix of aged soft cheese like camembert with butter, and seasonings such as paprika, and also a small amount of beer. This mixture is then spread on bread or pretzels.

90. Tour a Sumptuous Baroque Palace, Ludwigsburg Palace

About 12 kilometres outside of Stuttgart, you can find one of the grandest and most ornate palace complexes in Germany, Ludwigsburg Palace. This castle was constructed in the first half of the 18th century, and it's as interesting as it is beautiful. We think that the castle tour of Ludwigsburg Palace is one of the best we have ever been on. It tells the stories of the lives of the royals and the servants who lived there while walking through the beautiful rooms.

(Schlossstraße 30, 71634 Ludwigsburg; www.schloss-ludwigsburg.de)

91. Enjoy the Thrills and Spills of Europa-Park

Yes it's true that there are lots of museums to visit and lots of exciting things to do in Germany, but sometimes all you want to do is let loose and have a little bit of fun, right? Right. And that's when you find your way to Europa-Park, which is the largest amusement park in Germany, and the second largest in Europe following Disneyland Paris. The park is arranged into different parts of Europe, so you get to enjoy thrills and spills while learning about various European cultures.

(Europa-Park-Straße 2, 77977 Rust; www.europapark.de/en)

92. Stroll the Boxhagener Platz Market on the Weekend

If you want to find a bargain, it's always a good idea to head to the student area of any city, where the local students won't have much money. And right in the heart of Berlin's student quarter, you can find the Boxhagener Platz Market every single Sunday. This is a flea market where you can find anything and everything, so it's a good place to shop for kooky souvenirs. Unlike other markets in the city, this one runs late into the evening.

93. Tuck Into Currywurst After a Night Out

Every place in the world has its own version of drunk food. That one dish that is just so appealing when you've had one too many pints of beer and you have cravings for something savoury. In Germany, there are two drunk foods that you will routinely find. One is the doner kebab, which is, of course, originally from Turkey. And the other is currywurst, a kind of hot dog with ketchup that is flavoured with curry powder. It might not sound that appealing, but we are hooked.

94. Relax in the AlbThermen Spa of Bad Urach

Every now and then, it's important to give yourself permission to forget all about the various stresses of everyday life and to just enjoy the moment with a little bit of pampering. And when we feel like it's time to treat ourselves, we head to the AlbThermen Spa in the town of Bad Urach in Bavaria. The natural mineral springs will do you the world of good if you have tired feet from sightseeing, and the textile Turkish bath is a real treat too. *(http://albthermen.de/en)*

95. Visit the House of Richard Wagner

Germany has produced some of the best loved classical composers in music history. While you're in the country, it can be a great idea to take in a classical concert, but also to learn more about some of the most famous German composers. If you make it to the Bavaria region, stray away from Munich and head to Bayreuth where you can visit Richard Wagner's villa, Wahnfried. The house has been a museum since 1976, where you can learn more about the great man and his life in Bavaria.

(Richard-Wagner-Straße 48, 95444 Bayreuth; www.wagnermuseum.de)

96. Admire the Beautiful Berliner Dom

While Berliner is generally thought of as a cool city where you can check out the street art, go vintage shopping, and party the night away, there is another side to the city, because Berlin is a place with a long and glorious history. When you stand in front of Berliner Dom, or Berlin Cathedral, this is something that you can intuitively feel. If you can catch an organ recital inside the cathedral, don't let the opportunity pass you by.

(Am Lustgarten, 10178 Berlin; www.berlinerdom.de)

97. Take the Train From Munich to Innsbruck

Germany shares borders with an astounding nine European countries, which means that many people on a trip to Germany might also want to dip their toe into some other parts of Europe while they are there. From the southern city of Munich, you can take a direct train journey to Innsbruck in Austria, and this is a popular train journey for more than its usefulness. This train journey is extremely scenic, taking in the glistening lakes of Bavaria and Germany's highest mountain, Zugspitze.

98. Get a Caffeine Fix at the Berlin Coffee Festival

If you are the kind of person who can't start the day with a strong caffeine fix, fear not because you are most certainly not alone – Germany is a country full of coffee lovers. Of course, you can find great cafes all over the country, but if you are really devoted to coffee, we'd recommend a trip to the Berlin Coffee Festival, which is hosted each year at the beginning of September. You can expect tastings, food pairings, and even workshops in learning latte art. *(http://berlincoffeefestival.de)*

99. Indulge a Need for Speed at the Porsche Museum

Are you a car lover through and through? Then you absolutely need to head to the birthplace of Porsche automobiles, Stuttgart. Porsche have created a museum dedicated to their history, their technology, and the aesthetic beauty of their cars, which cost around 100 million euros to build. There are 80 or so exhibits within the museum that will take you through the whole lifespan of the brand.

(Porscheplatz 1, 70435 Stuttgart; www.porsche.com/museum/en)

100. Stay in a Fairtytale Treehouse at Baumhaus Hotel

If you would like to have a "back to nature" experience but you know yourself too well to camp in the outdoors and expose yourself to all kinds of creepy crawlies, the Baumhause Hotel in the German countryside could be right up your alley. This is a hotel with a set of eight treehouse rooms, that are deep in the forest and yet kitted out in luxury. There's also a medieval theatre on site with performances the whole family can enjoy.

(Seemühle 1, 97782 Gräfendorf; www.das-baumhaushotel.de)

101. Cycle Along the German Danube

The Danube is one of the most beloved rivers in Europe, running through Germany, Austria, Hungary, Serbia, and

Croatia, and its extraordinarily picturesque. It can be lovely to have a picnic on the side of the river, or simply walk along the riverbank. But our preferred way to explore this beautiful part of Germany is to cycle on the designated cycle path while taking in the gorgeousness of the Black Forest and the Franconian hills.

Before You Go…

Thanks for reading **101 Amazing Things to Do in Germany.** We hope that it makes your trip a memorable one!

Have a great trip, and don't drink too much German beer!

Team 101 Amazing Things

Printed in Germany
by Amazon Distribution
GmbH, Leipzig